March 2

Dear Susanne and Michel,

We hope you will leave Washington D.C
with many very happy memories.
The three of us, hope that the two
of you and your growing family
will often come and visit us here
in Virginia

Love always,

Patricia, Bill
Michael

WASHINGTON, D.C.

WASHINGTON, D.C.

Photography by
Kenneth Garrett

Introduction by
Bill Garrett

BOULTON

©1986 Boulton Publishing Services, Inc., Toronto

Designed by Fortunato Aglialoro
ISBN 0-920831-03-6
1 2 3 4 - 9 8 7 6
Printed in Hong Kong by Scanner Art Services, Inc., Toronto

Introduction

Like the heroine of *The Three Faces of Eve,* Washington lives with a split personality. Unlike Eve, Washington thrives on it.

There's the proper lady—the sedate, shaded city of wide lawns, old school and old money—the proper Eastern establishment city.

There's no obvious match for the drab housewife personality but there does exist what seems a shy, introverted personality, one that shuns the spotlight—and often for good reasons as we shall see.

The third—the face known best—is that of a world capital. She's a fast lady, a courtesan, a mistress—more the sequined gown than the gingham housedress type. More at home in a limousine than a pickup truck. She's a city born in a swamp beside Tiber Creek that has climbed a long way in a short time. She's still a young city that parties every night—a pretty city of wide avenues, her monumental elegance rouged with a blush of cherry blossoms in the spring—a seductive city, sometimes passionate but more often marked by small deceptions and occasionally by some of world-shaking consequence.

Tremendous power is focused on this 'village' by the Potomac. Like most elegant ladies, this Washington is drawn to power just as power is drawn to her. While other cities may deal in wheat, steel or electronics, and work up a sweat doing it, Washington's product is power, generated without mussing a pretty face with smoke and grime. Many Washingtonians agree with Henry Kissinger that 'power is the great aphrodisiac.'

Of course, like most things said in or about Washington, it isn't a new idea.

Powerful men and women gather in Washington from all over the world to deal in power. Lobbyists are drawn there to try to alter the flow of power with their charm, their connections and their favors. Many fail and become cynical. Some succeed and become powerful themselves.

Just as the 'three faces' of Eve made her memorable, so Washington's blur of personalities makes her one of the most exciting and important cities in the world.

Appropriately, the city is the offspring of a powerful man. George Washington personally chose the actual site in 1791 at the request of the Continental Congress, which had met in eight different cities and decided it needed a permanent home, one that would least offend the other rival cities. By 1800 things were far enough along for the new city to become the Capital of the United States. Congress named it in George Washington's honor. Washington chose Pierre Charles L'Enfant to lay out the plan. The French major immediately took the high ground—Jenkin's Hill—on which to put the Capitol, a rise for evermore to be known as Capitol Hill. The rest of the city was to be built to the east but rumor has it that power brokers had already moved in and speculators supposedly bought up the eastern plateau. Whatever the cause, the city grew towards the swamp on the west. In this case fate was more than kind. The Mall which leads west more than two miles from the foot of Capitol Hill makes Washington one of the most beautiful capitals in the world. But it wasn't always so. At first the humid swampy city attracted more mosquitoes and disease than people. For years Washington was considered to be a wilderness posting by the diplomatic corps.

Despite the foresighted brilliance of his plan, L'Enfant's name is a dirty word for those who try to drive in Washington for the first time. His circles and their radiating avenues make the city a maze of trapezoids and triangles that would rattle a homing pigeon.

There is no better way to meet Washington for the first time—or the thousandth—than to fly down the Potomac River from the northwest into National Airport. Be sure to get a seat on the left side and try to arrive when the city lights are on but the landscape is still bathed in the afterglow of sunset. You'll probably not see much of the river. It will usually be directly beneath the plane, the assumption being that the noise of jets arriving every other minute will aggravate the least number of people that way.

Once you clear the rolling green horse-country of Maryland and Virginia you'll glide past Georgetown at the head of tide and navigation. Until Congress abolished it as a 'separate and independent city' in 1895, Georgetown was the second oldest settlement in the area, serving since 1751 as the port of entry to and from the West. After it lost its separate legal identity, it suffered an eclipse and hard times but roared back to recovery after World War II and is now a prestigious address, with its little Federal row houses being among the most expensive residential real estate in the city.

Your plane will be moving too fast for you to see the little shops and restaurants that make Georgetown so popular, but you can't miss the spires of Georgetown University that crown the brow of the hill overlooking the Washington Canoe Club and the Chesapeake and Ohio Canal (now a National Park). The old Jesuit school is one of six Universities and four colleges in Washington that make education one of the few Washingtonian 'industries' outside government.

Hard on the southeastern edge of Georgetown and along the river bank sprawls the Watergate Apartment complex made famous by a failed break-in. Don't blink, as you fly along, because in the next few seconds you'll pass the Kennedy Center and the Lincoln Memorial. You are at about the same height above ground as the tourists in the lookout atop the Washington Monument.

To the north of the Monument you'll see the White House gleaming brightly. Built of Virginia stone, it was painted white to cover the black scars left after the British gutted it with fire in 1814. If you plan your time in Washington you can pay a visit to the President's house, and walk through elegant rooms where a few hours before diplomats, ministers, presidents and their ladies, kings and their consorts, may have been dining and dancing and working at the business of international diplomacy.

By now the wheels of the plane are down, but if you look back quickly your eye will naturally follow Pennsylvania Avenue to the east. When Charles Dickens visited Washington in 1842 he described this as one of the avenues that starts nowhere and leads nowhere. Now it leads from the most powerful legislative body on earth to the home of the most powerful man in the world.

A third of the way along the Avenue you'll probably notice the Old Post Office's 315-foot tower, the tallest structure in the city except for the Washington Monument. Saved from the wrecker's ball, and renamed The Nancy Hanks Center, this is now a thriving and varied complex.

At the end of Pennsylvania Avenue, high above the city and topped by a massive statue of Freedom, looms the awe-inspiring classical Capitol building.

In far less time than it took you to read this your plane will have touched down just two and a half miles from the Capitol building at National Airport—one of the most inadequate and exasperating but also one of the handiest airports in the world. Though many think the runways are too short and the approaches too dangerous for today's planes and the facilities inadequate for the crowds of travelers, Congressmen, who travel far too often for their physical health (in order to protect their political health), like the Airport and protect it because it is so convenient to their offices—only minutes away when the traffic isn't completely snarled.

If your bags arrive and a friendly relative or classmate doesn't, you'll need a taxi. If so, in the new few minutes you will very likely begin to meet another face of Washington—that seemingly shy, reclusive one. It's really about as shy as a gypsy and for the same reason. This is a city of itinerants, a way-station for the dispossessed, who may well be living here illegally. More than likely your taxi driver will be a member of the latest wave of refugees to seek out Washington. If you speak a mutual language you may find him or her to be one of the most interesting people you'll meet in the city though maybe needing help to find your destination.

On one trip my driver proved to be a former government minister from Afghanistan with a doctorate in economics. He had arrived in Washington flat broke and worked as a hack to support his family until he could land a job more suited to his skills—or maybe until he could get his papers in order.

In recent years Washington has seen waves of Iranians, Ethiopians, Southeast Asians, Afghans and other refugees arrive, each from the world's latest hot spot of the moment. Since 1979 between fifty and seventy thousand Hispanics arrived in Washington. The Adams-Morgan section is as Spanish now as Miami.

This is not a new phenomenon. Washington was one of the most important stops on the 'Underground Railroad'. Blacks from the south stopped here on their way north in great numbers, both before and after the Civil War. Seventy percent of the citizens of the District of Columbia and ninety-four percent of its children in public school are black. Over the years a reasonably integrated Federal City has evolved one of the largest middle-class black communities in the United States. The two mayors elected since Washington achieved 'home rule' in 1973 have both been black.

Most of the homeless who have arrived—from the indentured Englishman of colonial days to the latest Vietnamese boat person—bring talents and enthusiasm that are soon woven into the fabric of the city. They create a general ambience of international sophistication, and incidentally enrich Washington with one of the most remarkable ranges of excellent restaurants in the world.

Your driver will have had to cross one of the five bridges that connect Washington to Virginia. Ask him to stop at the Vietnam Veterans Memorial. It is the newest of the city's shrines and the one that generates the most emotional response. Just as Vietnam was controversial and divisive so was the black granite monument when it was built, but there are few who would deny that it has been a total success—a catalyst in helping to heal the nation's psychological wounds.

As you pass through town you'll notice that Washington's office skyscrapers don't scrape the sky. They huddle, shoulder-to-shoulder, like a military drill-team, all the same height, all toed up to the same sidewalk-line and all pretty monotonously alike. Building regulations require that no building compete with the Capitol dome. This leads builders to utilize every square foot of their lots. The newest National Geographic Society building created a bit of a sensation when the architect set it behind a small parklike entrance and did not shoot it straight up to maximum height.

In notable contrast to the often uninspired commercial architecture are the newest monumental additions to the Mall. The National Air and Space Museum—the most visited museum in Washington—affords its fabulous collection a grand hangar-like space in which to be enjoyed. Thanks to the leadership of former astronaut Michael Collins, the Museum's first director, this is one of the few government buildings in memory to be finished on time and within its budget. Across the Mall the new East Building of the National Gallery of Art gracefully and dramatically fills one of the trapezoid spaces created by L'Enfant's design. If there were any fault to be found with I.M. Pei's building it would only be that it overwhelms all but the grandest of works of art.

From one end of the Mall to the other you'll find a collection of fabulous galleries and museums—mostly Smithsonian—to satisfy almost every taste. If you've been walking the Mall, as you should to enjoy it to the full, you'll welcome the moving underground-sidewalk that connects the East Building to the West Building, with an inviting café and the Gallery's bookstore along the way. No matter how long you stay, you'll barely scratch the surface, so you might as well take a few books about Washington with you when you leave.

That is, *if* you leave. Many visitors contract 'Potomac fever' and never go home again. Henry Mitchell, a *Washington Post* columnist, got the fever when he arrived in Washington as a copyboy in 1949. In an article in *National Geographic* he wittily described the experience of millions of people since George Washington put the city on the map.

'Washington is the dreaming capital of America, stuffed with exiles who are always saying it's about time to go home but never go. The years turn into decades, and those who came for an extra year or two of school or for some temporary job, tend at the last to be carried out feet first with, I am obliged to report, a grin on the face.'

BILL GARRETT

1–3 The Cathedral Church of Saint Peter and Saint Paul, widely known as THE WASHINGTON NATIONAL CATHEDRAL. When completed, the Cathedral will be the sixth largest church in the world. This is a noble monument of the 14th century Gothic style, comparable in size and beauty to its French and English forebears. Work began in 1907, employing only medieval construction principles and materials, and has continued persistently since, despite the interruptions of wars and financial crises.

Though entrusted to Episcopalian governance, the Cathedral serves all denominations. It has no local membership or congregation of its own, but is open to all and depends upon the offerings of many affiliations. It has seen much history, moments of national mourning, vigil, thanksgiving and celebration, and is the last resting place of many famous Americans.

The Cathedral has been a setting for worship in every denomination and creed, so living up to its Charter from Congress, that it should be 'A House of Prayer for All People'. (See also plate 77.)

The tremendous ROSE WINDOW in the west facade of the NATIONAL CATHEDRAL (plate 2) represents the Seven Days of Creation. A north transept rose depicts the Last Judgement, and a south transept rose shows the Church Triumphant. The magnificence of the glass throughout the Cathedral is patterned after the glories of the French, such as Chartres and the Saint Chapelle in Paris. A distinctly modern touch is the Space Window, commemorating Apollo XI; embedded in the glass is a fragment of rock from the moon.

GEORGE WASHINGTON'S MARBLE STATUE glows with stained-glass light (plate 3). When Theodore Roosevelt laid the foundation stone of the National Cathedral in 1907 he used the same silver trowel as Washington used to set the Capitol cornerstone in 1793 and as was in turn used for the foundation of the Washington Monument in 1848.

The foundation stone of the Cathedral was a piece of American granite, in which was embedded a stone from a field at Bethlehem. Similarly the high altar is built of 12 stones from Solomon's quarry at Jerusalem. The pulpit is of stone from Canterbury, and the bishop's chair is of stone from Glastonbury, where King Arthur is said to have been buried.

4 (*left*) A classical view along the line of the Mall, axis of Washington's grand design. In front is THE LINCOLN MEMORIAL; behind to the left is THE WASHINGTON MONUMENT. In the distance, at the far end of the Mall is THE CAPITOL. Such a vista as this recalls the words with which historian Allan Nevins described the Capitol. It was 'the spirit of America in stone.' (See also plates 10, 11, 14–17, 68, 81, 85, 86.)

5 On display in THE NATIONAL ARCHIVES BUILDING, THE DECLARATION OF INDEPENDENCE, authored by Thomas Jefferson and signed by 56 representatives of the 13 United States at the Second Continental Congress in Philadelphia, 4 July 1776. One of Washington's most imposing classical buildings, the Archives (built in 1935) houses two centuries of historic records, including all major American treaties.

6 The most precious of all the treasures in THE NATIONAL ARCHIVES BUILDING are the three 'Charters of Freedom' —namely, the Declaration of Independence (see plate 5), THE CONSTITUTION OF THE UNITED STATES (seen here), and the Bill of Rights. These are on display every day to the public gaze but sheltered away at night by most elaborate security systems.

Signed on 17 September 1787 at the Constitutional Convention in Philadelphia, the Constitution was ratified first by Delaware, whose tribute stone in the Washington Monument reads 'First to Adopt, Will be the Last to Desert the Constitution.' New Hampshire, as the ninth state to sign, made up the required majority of two-thirds for acceptance and ratification.

7 The tribunal of final appeal and court of last resort for matters arising from the interpretation of state and federal laws in respect of their accordance with the Constitution, THE SUPREME COURT, together with the legislative and executive branches, is one of the three pillars of American government. The Court met in various parts of the Capitol building until, in 1935, the present Corinthian temple was built to the design of Architect Cass Gilbert.

The massive bronze doors of the western entrance weigh 3,000 pounds each and are cast in bas-relief panels, showing the development of law and justice in the western tradition, from Ancient Greece and Rome to Magna Carta and from Stuart England to the establishment of the American Republic.

Above the colonnaded entrance the Goddess of Liberty rules, with the scales of Justice on her lap. Below the pediment runs a great frieze with the words 'Equal Justice Under Law'. (See also plate 76.)

8 and 9 THE JEFFERSON MEMORIAL honors America's third President, author of the Declaration of Independence, father of the University of Virginia, one of the great spirits of his own or any age. Dedicated in 1943, that year being the two hundredth anniversary of Jefferson's birth, the memorial is of a kind that Jefferson himself admired and echoes his own designs for the University of Virginia and his own home, the beautiful Monticello.

Within the domed memorial is Rudolph Evans' heroic bronze statue and around the walls are four marble panels with inscriptions from Jefferson's writings. The circular frieze carries this promise from a letter of 1800: 'I have sworn on the altar of God, eternal hostility to every form of tyranny over the mind of man.' (See also plates 29 and 80.)

10 and 11 THE LINCOLN MEMORIAL 'In this temple, as in the hearts of the people for whom he saved the Union, the memory of Abraham Lincoln is enshrined forever.' So reads the inscription, above the figure of Lincoln, in this, the most revered of all the capital's monuments. The rectangular temple recalls the Parthenon of Athens, with the difference that the entrance is to the side, so that it can accent the end of the Mall and the Reflecting Pool, in perfect contrast to the soaring Washington Monument beyond. The marble statue of Lincoln by David Chester French is one of the most inspiring sculptures in the world. His hands resting on the arms of his chair, the President sits back in profound thought, looking out into the soul of the nation that he preserved. (See also plates 68 and 81.)

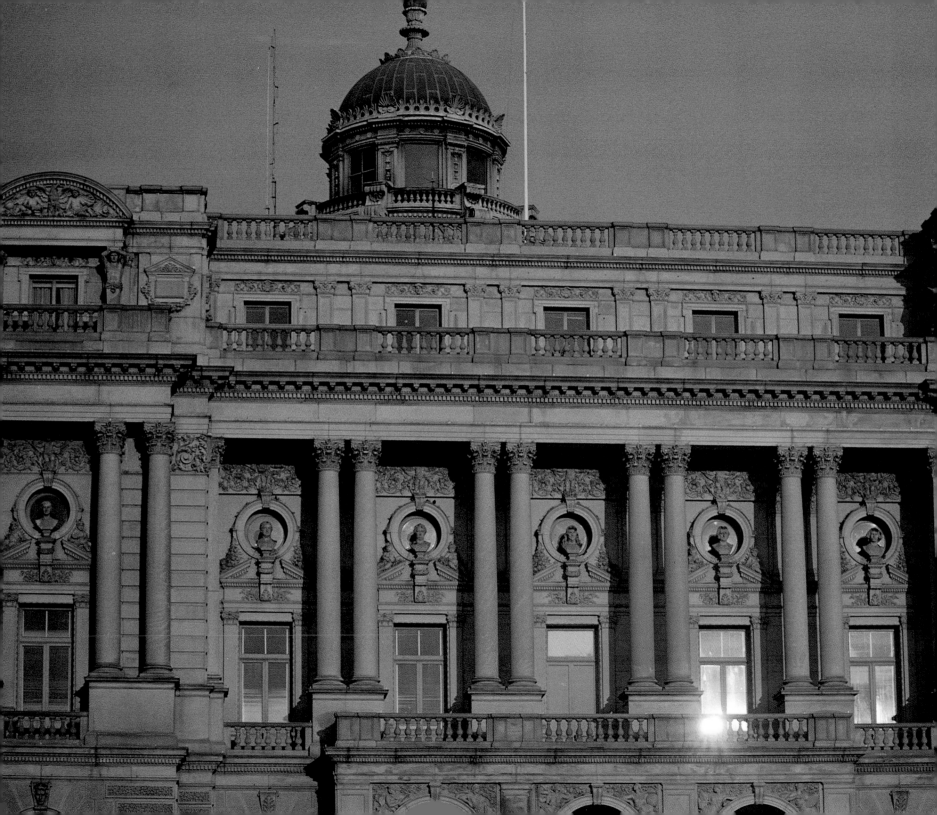

12 and 13 THE LIBRARY OF CONGRESS began in 1800 with Congressional funding of $5,000 in one room of the Capitol. It is now the largest library in the world. The original collection was lost when the Capitol was burned by the British in 1814. To replace it, the Congress acquired the private library of Thomas Jefferson, 6487 volumes for $23,950. The total complex today holds over 80 million items, including some of the richest collections in existence, from rare books to scientific books, from colonial records to Braille editions, from musical scores to early English legal material, from government documents to the Gutenberg Bible, from Hispanic, to Russian, to Chinese. . . . The list is endless and some 400 new items are added every hour.

The grand Main Building (plate 12) was opened in 1897, built in an ornate Italian Renaissance style reminiscent of the Paris Opera House; it was reckoned to be one of the most costly and beautiful buildings in the world at that time. Certainly it is magnificent, with murals and sculptures throughout. The heart of the Library is the Main Reading Room (plate 13) under the 160-foot-high dome.

14-17 George Washington laid the cornerstone of THE CAPITOL on
18 September 1793, but the square, two-storey building in which Congress
assembled in 1800 was a very humble forerunner of the palatial structure
that dominates the city now. The Capitol has evolved through two
centuries, most recently when the East Central Front was extended in
white Georgia marble. The huge cast-iron dome, weighing nine million
pounds (plate 17), was finished in 1863 with a bronze Statue of Freedom
on top, 278 feet above the ground. Completion of the dome was a symbol

of faith at that time. 'If people see the Capitol going on,' said Lincoln, 'it
is a sign we intend the Union shall go on.'

STATUARY HALL in The Old House Wing of the Capitol (plate 15) was
the Representatives' Chamber from 1807 to 1857. Though some of the
American government's most dramatic moments were lived out here, the
overcrowding and impossible acoustics (better suited to a whispering
gallery) led to the chamber's abandonment. It was even used for a time
as a market-place, until in 1864 it was cleared out and dedicated as

'Statuary Hall' to which each State might send statues of distinguished citizens. In time the room became overcrowded with statues and these spilled out into nearby corridors and the Hall of Columns. Since 1933 each State has been limited to one statue in the Hall.

THE GREAT ROTUNDA of the Capitol (plate 16) is an immense circular hall, 96 feet across and more than 183 feet from the floor to the top. A monument of architectural genius, the work of Thomas U. Walter of Philadelphia, the Rotunda, like many other parts of the Capitol, is decorated with Constantine Brumidi's frescoes depicting the virtues and history of the Republic. Like Michelangelo before him, Brumidi worked on a scaffold far above the ground. A terrifying fall led to his death in 1880, leaving the work only one third completed. The last panels were filled in as late as 1953. In addition to the frescoes the Rotunda is distinguished by Trumbull's paintings of the Revolutionary War.

Lincoln was the first of many great Americans whose bodies have lain in state here, others among them being the Unknown Soldier of World War I and President John F. Kennedy. (See also plates 66 and 88.)

18 and 19 Gilbert Stuart's portraits of the first three Presidents, Washington, Adams and Jefferson, hang in THE NATIONAL GALLERY OF ART. Owing its existence to Andrew Mellon's donation of his own magnificent collection, the Gallery was opened as recently as 1941, but has established itself as one of the finest museums in the world. It is especially strong in nineteenth century European paintings and in Italian Renaissance masterpieces, including the only Leonardo da Vinci outside Europe.

Entered through bronze doors from the Mall, the great round hall of the National Gallery, 100 feet in diameter and 100 feet high to its dome, is the central core of the building's palatial design.

20 and 21 Architect I.M. Pei's marble masterpiece, THE EAST BUILDING OF THE NATIONAL GALLERY OF ART, is one of Washington's most popular attractions. The pink marble from Tennessee matches that of the classical main building in two great interlocking triangles designed to fit the unusual shape of the site. Although much of the East Building is given to special exhibits, ranging from Rodin to the Aztecs, there are some permanent favorites here, among them Alexander Calder's massive 920-pound mobile, which dominates the handsome central atrium of the East Building.

22 (*above*) A chamber orchestra provides background music in THE EAST BUILDING OF THE NATIONAL GALLERY to an opening-night reception for members of Congress.

23 (*right*) THE JOHN F. KENNEDY CENTER FOR THE PERFORMING ARTS is a national cultural center built on a scale so vast that the Washington Monument could be laid down lengthwise in the Grand Foyer with room to spare. The Center holds a 2,200-seat Opera House that also offers musical comedy, ballet and modern dance; a Concert Hall with the National Symphony Orchestra that also hosts visiting orchestras, choirs and soloists; The Terrace Theater for a variety of music, dance and cabaret; and the American Film Institute for everything most memorable of the movies. The Center is a masterpiece in itself, the work of the architect Edward Durrell Stone.

24 (*left*) PENNSYLVANIA AVENUE in the evening; looking from Western Park towards the Capitol Building.

25 Eero Saarinen designed this huge architectural marvel, THE TERMINAL BUILDING AT DULLES INTERNATIONAL AIRPORT, Chantilly, Virginia, just to the southwest of Washington. It was dedicated by President Kennedy in 1962 in memory of John Foster Dulles, historic Secretary of State (1953–59) in the Eisenhower administration. Saarinen's design seems to contain an energy that is striving to leap from the ground. It is widely admired as one of the outstanding buildings of its kind in the world.

26 (*left*) Washington is home to THE HEADQUARTERS OF THE NATIONAL GEOGRAPHIC SOCIETY, whose permanent exhibition in Explorers' Hall tells the story of nearly a century's exploration and discovery around the world. The largest free-standing globe in existence is only one of the fascinating subjects on display here. The Society's headquarters building was designed by the architect Edward Durrell Stone, who also designed the Kennedy Center. Set behind a small park-like entrance, this is yet another of Washington's handsome modern buildings. Here we see high-tech cartography in progress.

27 Space telescope being assembled at the NATIONAL AERONAUTICS AND SPACE ADMINISTRATION.

28 UNION STATION was completed in 1907 in the grand tradition of classic Beaux-Arts European railway termini. It has one of Washington's most immense interiors. In 1968 legislation changed it into a visitors' center and it was opened as such for the Bicentennial but, after much controversy, immense costs, and major repairs, plans are now under way to get the grand old station back on the rails.

29 (*right*) The beautiful white single-flowering Japanese cherry blossoms around THE TIDAL BASIN are the first to appear in late March or early April. A Japanese stone lantern is lighted to begin The Cherry Blossom Festival, usually held in the first week or ten days of April, with a pageant, a parade, and the Coronation of the Cherry Blossom Queen. In the background the Jefferson Memorial shines in the sun. (See also plates 8, 9, 80.)

30 Evening light on the rails of the METRO
SWITCHING YARDS at Lanham, Maryland.

31 (*right*) WESTERN PLAZA ON PENNSYLVANIA
AVENUE, below 13th and 14th Streets NW,
commemorates the design laid out by Major
Pierre Charles l'Enfant for the Capital of the
young republic. A geometric grid is modified by
the Renaissance device of having several streets
diverge from a single point, resulting in a pattern
of diagonals overlaid on a chequer board. The
purpose was to create grand avenues, parks and
squares, with multiple vistas and long, architectural perspectives, the eighteenth century's ideal
of a ruling city. Despite later plans and modifica-
tions and the pressures of modern construction
and automobiles, L'Enfant's plan remains the
framework that gives Washington its sense of
space and timeless grandeur. (See also plate 82.)

32 The west-end riverfront of the Potomac has grown rapidly since the building of the Kennedy Center and THE WATERGATE COMPLEX, seen here directly beyond the State Department, which is itself the second-largest building belonging to the US government.

33 (*right*) CRYSTAL CITY, looking across to the Washington Monument.

34 Pershing Plaza's summer fountain becomes a winter playground, especially at lunchtime. In the background looms THE TREASURY BUILDING, dating from 1838–42, when it replaced a previous building that burned in 1833. President Andrew Jackson required that it be next to the White House. Pierre l'Enfant's plan had provided for a 'Grand Avenue' leading directly without interruption from the Capitol to the White House. There was so much debate and delay over where to put the new Treasury that finally 'Old Hickory' lost patience, stalked out of the White House one morning, stuck his cane in the ground and said '*This* is where I want the cornerstone!' As a result all parades must sidestep the Treasury.

35 (*right*) The former APEX THEATER, that once housed the photographic darkroom of the legendary Matthew Brady, has recently been completely overhauled and renovated by SEARS ROEBUCK as their WORLD TRADE HEADQUARTERS.

36 Forerunner of THE ORGANIZATION OF AMERICAN STATES, the Pan-American Union built this handsome palace of white marble in 1908–10, largely with the contributions of Andrew Carnegie. The building has beautiful gardens both inside and outdoors, a Hall of the Americas, a Hall of Flags and Heroes, a Columbus Memorial Library, as well as statuary, murals and architectural decorations indicative of the histories and cultures of the member countries. The OAS, representing the 21 republics of the Americas, is the oldest international organization in the world.

37 LOOKING DOWN THE MALL from the foot of Capitol Hill.

38 (*left*) THE NATIONAL AIR AND SPACE MUS-EUM, opened in 1976, is one of Washington's principal tourist attractions and one of the most popular museums in the world. The museum tells the story of man in the air and in space, from the Wright Brothers' *Kitty Hawk* to Lindbergh's *Spirit of St Louis* to the *Apollo II* Command Module. There are 23 galleries of dramatic exhibits (see plates 42–45) and a cinema with a screen five stories high. In 1984 the National Air and Space Museum had ten million visitors.

39 James Smithson's crypt and tomb lie just off the entrance to THE SMITHSONIAN BUILDING. In 1829 this Englishman, who had never even been to America, died leaving his fortune of $500,000 to the United States for use in the spread of scientific knowledge. It took Congress until 1846 to decide what to do with the bequest; at length it created the Smithsonian Institution as a government foundation charged, among other things, with the custody of all national museum collections. The Smithsonian embraces the Museum of History and Technology, Natural History, Air and Space (see plate 38 opposite), the Astrophysical Observatory, the National Zoological Park, the National Collection of Fine Arts, the National Museum of American History, the National Gallery, and the Kennedy Center, as well as major collections, research facilities, information exchanges, and publishing services.

40 and 41 THE NATIONAL MUSEUM OF AMERICAN HISTORY memorializes 'everyday life in the American past' from the times of George Washington (whose false teeth are here) to that of Nancy Reagan (whose white satin dress is here). Along the way are to be seen thousands of fascinating artefacts and environments, model ships, an enormous locomotive, rare stamps, an 1861 Post Office, a 1900s candy store, the original Star-Spangled Banner, and a pendulum that lets you watch the earth revolve.

Here are two of the Smithsonian's collection of vintage automobiles—a 1932 Ford on the left and a 1927 Packard on the right.

42 and 43 THE NATIONAL AIR AND SPACE MUSEUM houses many historic aircraft. (See plate 38.) Here on the left in plate 42 is a scene on the French airfield at Verdun in World War I. An American Spad VII is flying upside down above a captured German Fokker D VII.

On the right (plate 43) is the original US Air Force X-15 hanging in the central hall of the National Air and Space Museum.

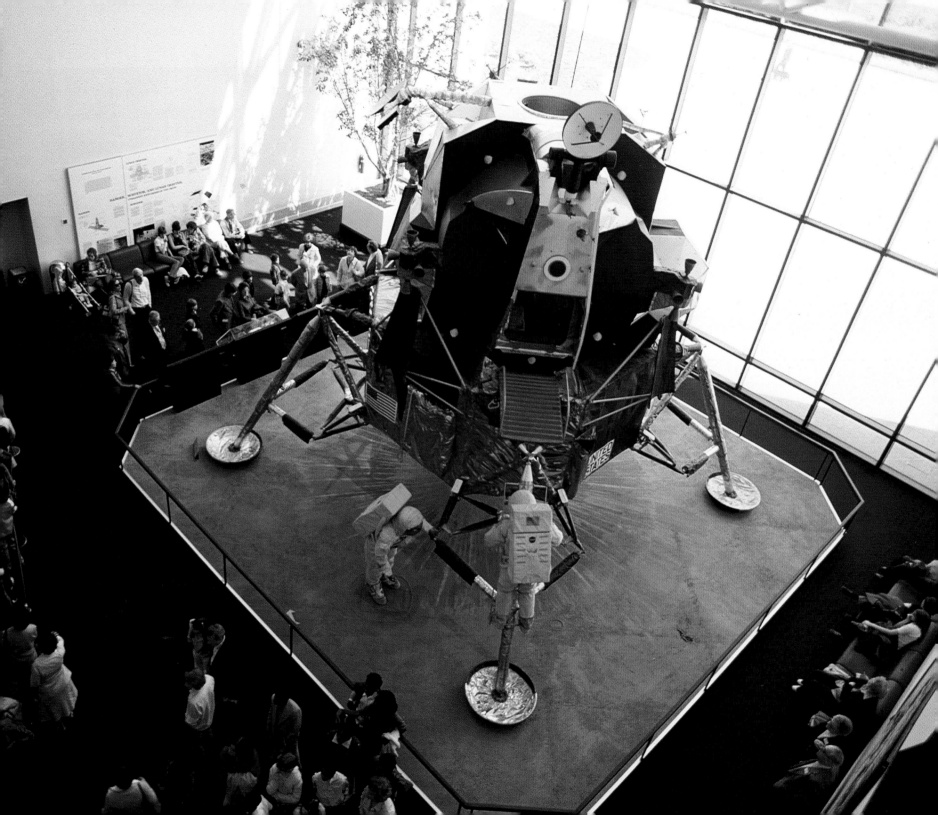

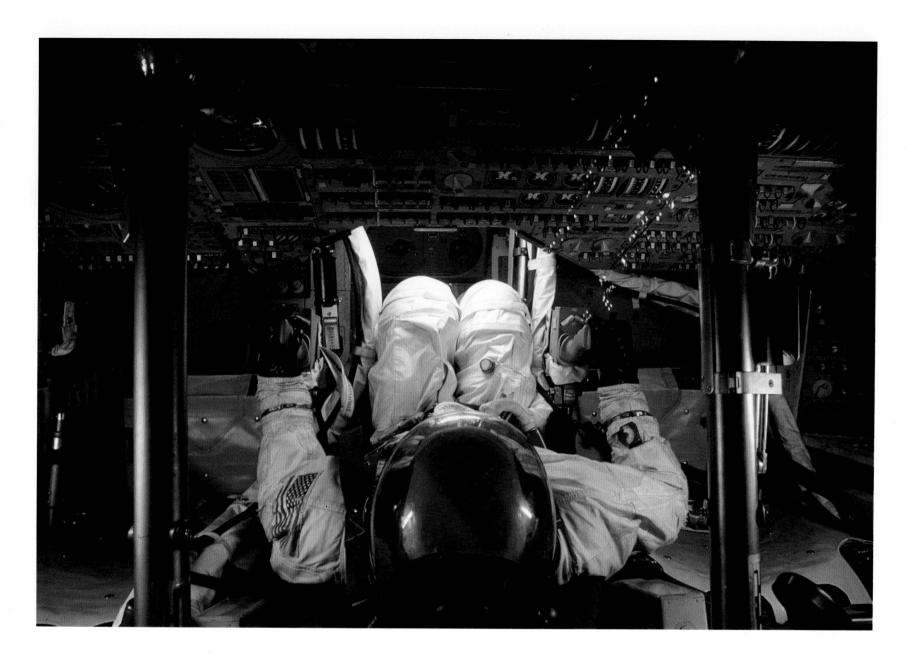

44 and 45 Another highlight of THE NATIONAL AIR AND SPACE MUSEUM
is the replica of the Apollo lunar landing module (plate 44), identical to the
one from which the first mortal step was made on the moon.
Plate 45 shows us inside the Apollo capsule.

46 THE SMITHSONIAN BUILDING, popularly known as 'THE CASTLE', was built of red-brick and sandstone in 1852 to house the headquarters of the Smithsonian Institution. A medley of towers and pinnacles in Victorian-Norman style, the Castle contains in its great hall an 'index exhibit' showing the vast scope of the Institution's work and of its 30-million-item collections. Also in the Castle are the Smithsonian Library and headquarters for Smithsonian publications.

Here the late evening lights glow from the Castle windows and the Capitol dome gleams beyond.

47 Cobblestones and streetcar tracks are preserved on only a few streets in Georgetown—challenging motorists to 'ride the rails' or hobble down the cobbles.

47–55 First incorporated as the town of George and then again as George Town and now an adjunct of the capital, GEORGETOWN goes back to 1751. By the time of Independence it was a flourishing center of trade with a busy seaport and the largest tobacco market in the Union. By the early nineteenth century the great inland canals, the mills and markets of 'GeorgeTown' and a world-wide traffic of shipping promised a commercial metropolis second to none. Instead, steamships demanded deeper

harbors and railroads made the great canals obsolete. Gradually George Town lost its importance and its wealth.

Meanwhile the city of Washington grew in dominance and in 1895 the two were merged in one. 'Georgetown' (as by then it was generally known) became a pleasant but somewhat neglected suburb of the capital city alongside.

In their first heyday the slopes of Georgetown were built upon by wealthy merchants whose classical Georgian mansions and rows of Federal townhouses have found a new lease on life in recent decades. Trim, dignified, well-proportioned fronts are graced by elegant details, finely-worn shutters, wrought-iron railings, brass trim and delicate carved-wood finishing touches. Brick sidewalks are shady with trees. Some streets still have cobblestones.

THE CHESAPEAKE AND OHIO (C&O) CANAL (plate 49) was begun in 1828 and opened up trade-links for Georgetown from the Great Lakes to the Gulf. Now just a quiet inland waterway, the Canal is maintained by the National Parks Service and instead of freight carries canoeists and vacationers. Joggers enjoy its footpath in the mornings.

48 A peaceful flag, waving over this historic Georgetown house, reminds one of a simpler day when the carriage house out back housed a carriage, and the driver took the horses down the road to the livery stable.

49 (*right*) The historic C&O canal provides a backbone for much of the restoration and growth in today's Georgetown.

50 (*left*) This brick and shutter style dominates Georgetown's historic row houses.

The old houses of Georgetown are in great demand. Easy distances mean simply walking home at the end of the day for many who work in the capital. Some of the handsome mansions hide beautiful gardens within the privacy of their old brick walls.

51 PISCES is one of Georgetown's most exclusive private clubs.

Georgetown is rich in restaurants, nightclubs, art galleries, bookstores, boutiques, private clubs, small luxurious hotels (such as THE LOMBARDY, plate 53), and exclusive shopping malls (such as GEORGETOWN PARK, plates 52 and 54). It has the vigour of London's Chelsea with the grace and class of Charleston. Georgetown has no national memorials, no

monumental centers of government power —though it may be some of those sheltered gardens and shuttered dining-rooms see as much action as the corridors of Congress. Yet, private, elegant, artistic and above all peaceful, George-town can fairly claim to be Washington's most seductive part of all.

52 Inside Georgetown Park's shopping mall one finds only the most exclusive items.

53 The Lombardy Hotel is a small inn appealing to the business traveler.

54 Georgetown Park is the newest Boutique Style shopping mall in the area.

55 The classical row houses of Georgetown are among the most exclusive and expensive residential real estate in Washington.

56 (*left*) Founded by Belgian-trained Jesuit John Carroll in 1789, GEORGE-
TOWN UNIVERSITY is the oldest Roman Catholic university college in
the United States. Its medieval Gothic spires dominate Georgetown from
the Potomac bluffs. Ironically, Archbishop Carroll chose the Georgetown
site over what is now Capitol Hill because he thought the latter would be
too far out 'in the country'.

57 HEADQUARTERS BUILDING OF *USA TODAY,*
ROSLYN

58 THE PENTAGON consists of five concentric rings of buildings that together house the population and facilities of a sizeable small town. This was the largest office building in the world when it was built in 1943. It is the principal headquarters of US Defense, Army, Navy, Air Force and Joint Chiefs of Staff.

59 (*right*) Federal government buildings line CONSTITUTION AVENUE. In the foreground the shadow of the Washington Monument moves round like that on a sun-dial. In the middle distance rises the tower of the Old Post Office Building. (See plate 78.)

60 THE HEADQUARTERS OF THE AMERICAN RED CROSS exemplifies
the ideals and the history of the Red Cross in statuary, Tiffany stained-
glass windows, and museum exhibits housed in three handsome classical
buildings of white marble. The Red Cross Museum vividly portrays the
service of the Red Cross in World War I and the bronze 'Statue of a
Nurse' in the courtyard commemorates those of the Red Cross who
gave their lives in the course of the conflict.

61 (right) THE NAVY AND MARINE MEMORIAL on Columbia Island
catches the eyes of travellers returning to the city from National Airport.
The sculpture portrays seven seagulls above a breaking wave, an illusion
of flight being achieved by joining the birds at their wingtips.

62 (*left*) The new WASHINGTON, D.C. CONVENTION CENTER, opened in 1983, has at last enabled the capital to house even the very largest conventions and in so doing has given a great impetus to downtown growth in the hotel and restaurant industry.

63 THE WASHINGTON SQUARE BUILDING is a distinctive new feature of the legal district. Not surprisingly, Washington has more lawyers per capita of population than any other city in the United States.

64 SHERIDAN CIRCLE, across Rock Creek from Georgetown, is right at the heart of Washington's diplomatic district, with several embassies around the Circle itself that in turn gives onto 'Embassy Row' with many more embassies located on Massachusetts Avenue.

65 (*right*) THE NATIONAL SHRINE OF THE IMMACULATE CONCEPTION was conceived as the greatest Roman Catholic church in the Western Hemisphere and is indeed one of the most impressive basilicas in the world. Parishes throughout America contributed to its building, as did Popes, Cardinals, Catholic Associations, and gifts from scores of countries. The church was 39 years in construction before it was dedicated in 1959, but the concept goes back much farther than that, indeed for a century and more. Now the Shrine is truly a Church for all Roman Catholics throughout America and beyond.

66 (*left*) FULL MOON OVER THE CAPITOL By day the sunlight is brilliant on the central dome, which is painted white to bring the cast-iron into harmony with the marble of the building. By night the dome is floodlit. A single light burns in the lantern when Congress is in session. (See also plates 14–17.)

67 MOUNT VERNON was inherited by George Washington a few years before he married Martha Custis and from then until his death in 1799 he was devoted to the improvement, expansion and management of the estate, leaving his beloved home with reluctance and then only to answer his call first as Commander of the Revolutionary Armies and later for eight years as President. Thanks to the generosity of the Mount Vernon Ladies Association in 1858 and ever since the manor house and its grounds have been restored and preserved for all the people.

68 (*left*) LINCOLN MEMORIAL 'With malice toward none; with charity for all; with firmness in the right, as God gives us to see the right, let us strive on to finish the work we are in; to bind up the nation's wounds; to care for him who shall have borne the battle, and for his widow, and his orphan....' from the *Second Inaugural Address* (see also plates 10, 11, 81.)

69 ARLINGTON: THE CUSTIS-LEE MANSION AND THE KENNEDY FLAME The Arlington estate was founded by John Parke Custis, son of Martha Washington by her first marriage. His son (Martha's grandson) George Washington Parke Custis, was adopted by Washington when John Custis died. George Custis built the mansion known as Arlington House in 1817. It descended to Martha's great grand-daughter Mary and in 1831 the parlor was the scene of her marriage to a young West Point graduate and lieutenant of the cavalry, Robert E. Lee. Thirty years later Mary's husband, by then a colonel, sat in his home at Arlington agonising over Lincoln's invitation to command the Union army about to invade Virginia. 'I can anticipate no greater calamity than the dissolution of the Union,' he wrote; but 'a union that can only be maintained by swords and bayonets...has no charm for me.' He resigned his commission, left the house at Arlington, never to return, and rode into history as the noble Commander of the Confederate South.

Down the slope from the Mansion is the grave of President John F. Kennedy. The everlasting flame was lit by his widow on the day of his burial, 25 November 1963, and by day or night can be seen from afar. (See also plate 72 and 75.)

70 US MARINE CORPS WAR MEMORIAL, ARLINGTON On 23 February 1945 American marines with the US Fifth Fleet captured Mount Surabachi on the Island of Iwo Jima. The battle, that was critical to the final assault on Japan, claimed 6,855 lives from the Navy and the Marines and 21,000 wounded. Joseph Rosenthal's Pulitzer-Prize-winning photograph captured the moment when a group of Marines raised Old Glory on the mountain. Felix de Weldon's immense bronze statue preserves that moment forever in a memorial to all United States Marines. The flag is a real one, not a piece of statuary, and by unique Presidential order it is never lowered at sundown, but flies on through the night.

71 The Silent Drill Team and the Drum and Bugle Corps beat the Retreat
on a summer evening at the BARRACKS OF THE US MARINES.

AND SO MY FELLOW AMERICANS
ASK NOT WHAT YOUR COUNTRY CAN DO FOR YOU
ASK WHAT YOU CAN DO FOR YOUR COUNTRY
MY FELLOW CITIZENS OF THE WORLD · ASK NOT `
WHAT AMERICA WILL DO FOR YOU · BUT WHAT TOGETHER
WE CAN DO FOR THE FREEDOM OF MAN

72 (*left*) 'JOHN FITZGERALD KENNEDY, 1917–1963' Facing the Kennedy graves, those of the President, his two infant children, and his brother Robert, is a low sloping wall in which are carved the words of President Kennedy's 1961 Inaugural Address. They were chosen by Mrs Kennedy and now, along with the words commemorated in Washington's other Presidential memorials, they have taken their place in the lore and language of modern Western man.

73 THE VIETNAM VETERANS MEMORIAL is not the only one of Washington's monuments that stirred controversy when new. The Washington Monument, the Jefferson Memorial, the Lincoln Memorial, the Kennedy Grave all had their antagonists, and all have found their place in the hearts of Americans and the friends of American ideals around the world. And so it is, after a decade of self-doubt, that this memorial by Maya Lin, dedicated in 1982 to 58,055 Americans killed in Vietnam between 1959 and 1975, has become a national shrine with 100,000 visitors a week. Most parish churches and many village memorials have their Rolls of Honor. Uniquely among national war memorials the Vietnam Veterans Memorial lists each of the fallen by name. The two solemn triangular walls of black granite, set at an angle and going down to meet each other at a central vertex, draw the visitor into an intensely personal encounter.

74 Washington is rich in symbolic ironies. The hillside that was to become THE ARLINGTON NATIONAL CEMETERY received its first graves late in the Civil War, when part of the former Robert E. Lee estate was set aside as a burial ground for the Union dead. Yet the first to be buried there was a Confederate who had died in hospital. The vast majority of the early graves were those of refugee black volunteers who had enlisted with the Union armies early in the Civil War. Arlington today is the last resting-place of Americans by the hundred thousands, from all the wars, including the Unknown Soldiers of World War I, World War II, the Korean War and the Vietnamese War. Here also are the graves of John and Robert Kennedy, General Pershing, General Marshall, and many other distinguished Americans including, to introduce a less solemn

note, Major Pierre Charles L'Enfant, the French engineer from the Revolutionary War who designed and laid out the beautiful city of Washington.

75 LOOKING DOWN FROM ARLINGTON One day in early 1963, only a few months before his death, President John Kennedy visited Arlington, and stood on the grass slope just below the Mansion. Looking out over the prospect of Washington shining in the clear spring sunlight, he turned to a friend and said, 'I could stay here forever.'

From the Kennedy flame the view looks down across the low arches of the Arlington Memorial Bridge to the response of the Lincoln Memorial and it is Lincoln's words at Gettysburg that speak as well for Arlington '...that from these honored dead we take increased devotion to that cause for which they gave their last full measure of devotion....'

76 Stunning in its Greco-Roman splendor, THE
SUPREME COURT BUILDING yet drew some
crusty comments at first when compared with
earlier and simpler quarters. One suggestion was
that the justices 'should enter such precincts on
elephants.'

Especially attractive today is the color of the
stone at sunrise and sunset, when the shadows in
the white Vermont marble take on the creamy
color of rose petals.

77 (*right*) Set on a magnificent site, Mount St
Alban, 400 feet above the Potomac, THE WASH-
INGTON NATIONAL CATHEDRAL dominates the
northwest skyline. At 676 feet above sea-level
the *Gloria in Excelsis* tower is the highest point
in Washington. The tower was begun in 1961. It
carries a 53-bell carillon with a peal of ten bells
capable of ringing more than three million
different changes. (See also plates 1-3.)

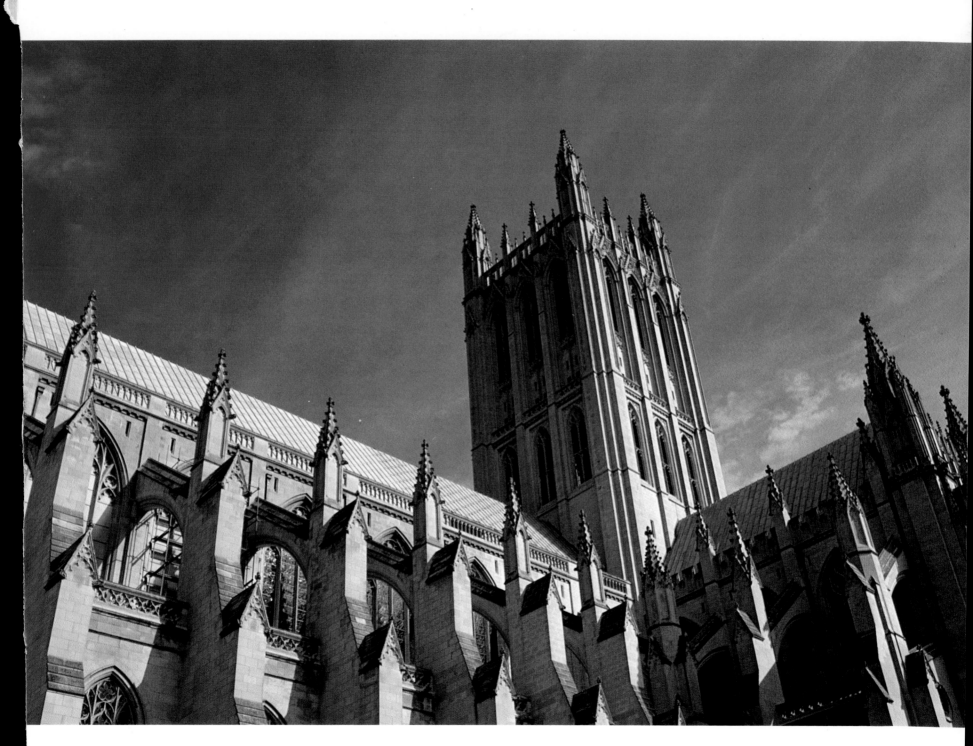

78 (*left*) The tower of THE OLD POST OFFICE BUILDING, 315 feet high, is the tallest structure in the city except for the Washington Monument. The Romanesque building was threatened with demolition for redevelopment a few years ago but was spared through the efforts of a public protest inspired by the late Nancy Hanks, head of the National Endowment for the Arts under Presidents Nixon and Ford. Renamed the Nancy Hanks Center, the once dingy Post Office is now a focus of activity on Pennsylvania Avenue. A good plan, a lot of spit-and-polish, and 30 million dollars have converted it into an attractive complex of offices, restaurants and shops. The grand 11-storey atrium has an elevator that carries 30,000 visitors a month up to the clock-tower lookout that is operated by the National Parks Service. The tower holds the only replicas ever cast of the bells of Westminster Abbey, a gift from Great Britain at the time of the Bicentennial.

79 Looking down the still waters of THE REFLECTING POOL towards the Lincoln Memorial. At other times the Pool attracts model boats, hopeful fishermen and even skaters in winter.

80 (*left*) Night falls on THE JEFFERSON MEMORIAL. The Tidal Basin creates another of the many classical vistas that call to mind the ancient Mediterranean world. Here is the perfect setting for the Memorial, reflected in water and framed by trees. (See also plates 8, 9, 29.)

81 Each of the 36 Doric columns of THE LINCOLN MEMORIAL stands for one of the 36 member States of the Union at the time of Lincoln's death. Their names appear on the frieze above, and on the parapet are those of the 48 States that comprised the Union when the memorial was completed in 1922. (See also plates 10, 11, 68.)

82 (*left*) THE MALL, central axis of Major Pierre Charles L'Enfant's original design for the capital of the young Republic, here seen looking east towards Capitol Hill. (See also plate 31.)

83 and 84 Nobody knows for certain how THE WHITE HOUSE came to be so-called, whether from its Virginia sandstone, or from its shining paint, or from Southern Plantation tradition. First called the President's Palace, then officially known as the Executive Mansion for nearly a hundred years, the White House is indeed a palace, small but elegant, set in landscaped grounds that would grace a ducal home in Europe. First constructed in 1792, the White House has gone through many alterations and additions since, until between 1948 and 1952 it was entirely rebuilt from within, the greatest care being taken to restore the interior to its original beauty. Today the White House reflects the changing times and tastes of all the Presidents and First Ladies who have lived there, which is to say everyone except George and Martha Washington. The authentic traditional beauty of the White House interior today owes much to the work of Mrs John F. Kennedy who restored it as an exquisite monument of living history.

84 (*left*) The White House.

85 and 86 The history of THE WASHINGTON MONUMENT
is almost as old as the Republic itself. As early as 1783 the
Continental Congress wanted 'an equestrian statue' and a
place was made for it in the plans for the capital, but the
expenditure was vetoed as wasteful excess by Washington
himself. The search for a monument looked at various
forms and suffered many setbacks, among them public
apathy, sectarian strife and the Civil War. Work began in

1848 on a cornerstone set with the same trowel that George Washington had used to lay the Capitol cornerstone in 1793. Finally in the 1880's, thanks to George P. Marsh, the US Ambassador to Italy, the monument was reconceived on the classical Egyptian design of an unaccompanied obelisk with a height ten times the length of the baseline. The solid aluminum tip was placed in 1884, crowning the tallest structure in the world. Even now the 55-story Monument remains the tallest of all masonry structures and commands an unrivalled position in Washington thanks to the building restriction that holds all other structures to a 13-storey limit. Indeed so high does the hollow shaft of stone reach up that condensation sometimes rains inside at the upper levels.

Inside the shaft are many inscribed blocks of stone contributed to the Monument by the member States of the Union and by scores of foreign nations, among them the 'Mormon State of Deseret' as Utah was still called then, and California which describes itself as 'the youngest sister of the Union', and the Sultanate of Turkey, and the Hanseatic Free City of Bremen, names that speak of a vanished age. Now just entering its second century, the Washington Memorial is the focal centerpiece for all the glories of this capital city and stands as a symbol of the ideals on which the Republic was founded, and in which it has endured.

87 (*right*) THE NATIONAL CHRISTMAS TREE ON THE WHITE HOUSE LAWN